AURAS

THEIR MEANING *and* MAGIC

GAIA ELLIOT

Quadrille

PART I

✦

PART II

PART

· I ·

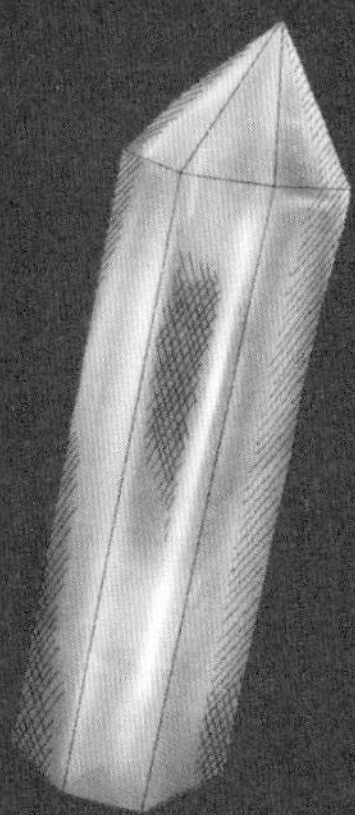

Introduction

In Greek, the noun 'aura' means a breeze or fresh air and in Middle English 'aura' meant a puff of air or a gentle wind. Over time, 'aura' came to mean an atmosphere, a sense of some subtle presence or idea, such as the aura of warmth that comes from our friendship with and love for another person. It's a sensitivity or awareness that we can learn to rely on and trust.

Each of us also has an individual aura, a form of physical energy that connects us to the energy all around us: the energy of other people, the environment in which we live, and the universe itself. Like everyone else, you have an energy field with its own vibrational levels that connects your body to your feelings, your spiritual heart and your cosmic being. This energetic field is your aura, and everyone's aura is completely individual to them. As with any vibrational energy, your aura can fluctuate. Some days, you feel vibrant and connected, as if you're firing on all cylinders. On other days, you may feel less focused, more contemplative, more low-key. And if you are physically unwell, you may be aware that your energy is low, possibly stagnant or blocked.

While auras are invisible to many, some psychics and holistic health practitioners can see the type, colour and vibrational energy of someone's aura. They can tell from the aura alone whether that person's energy is balanced or blocked, healthy or in need of adjusting. Sometimes, what's not obvious to you is very clear to an aura reader, and they may be able to help or advise you.

Everything has an aura, whether it's an animal, a plant or even a crystal. Although the idea of aura energy can seem rather abstract, esoteric or metaphysical, once we become aware of it, we can learn to see it, revitalise it and tap in to its power for our own constructive use. We can learn how to see and feel this energy, and how to balance and strengthen it. Learning more about it is just the first step, but this knowledge can be powerful, informing the way we choose to act towards, react to and interact with others. A knowledge of your aura is genuinely beneficial, something you can access when you need to 'power up' – and this book will show you how.

The Seven Auras

The auric field surrounds the physical body and is made up of seven auras or layers of energy. Each layer vibrates with its own energetic frequency; the lower the frequency, the closer to the body. Each of the auras relates to one of the seven chakras of the body, and resonates with the same colour. The highest auric frequency relates to the causal body and to the crown chakra (see page 41), while the lowest vibrating frequency relates to the physical body and the root chakra (see page 53).

The Physical Body

This is the red layer of auric energy closest to your skin (see page 10). Here is where you may feel your skin prickle in response to a change in atmosphere, or the hairs rise on the back of your neck: sensations we have all experienced and can recognise.

This aura is connected to your root chakra (see page 53).

The Emotional Body

This orange layer (see page 10) relates to your feelings; whether you're happy, sad or depressed, it will show up here. You may feel things in your gut as a physical response to an emotion. Our intuition often starts as a gut response; you may sense a vibe or an indication of something different, whether positive or negative.

This aura is connected to your sacral chakra (see page 51).

The Mental Body

This yellow layer (see page 10) is the level of rational and intellectual reasoning, and it's where we are at our most logical. We often use our reason to cut through the energy of reaction, to pause and harness our intellectual ability to make sense of what we see and feel. It's one of the greatest human abilities: to take a gut reaction, then evaluate and respond to it.

This aura is connected to your solar plexus chakra (see page 49).

The Astral Body

This is the green layer (see page 10) where our capacity for love functions at a spiritual level. You may sense this aura when you meet a much-loved friend, when your child hurts their knee and you *feel* their pain, or when your eyes meet those of a potential lover across a crowded room. This aura can also connect the body and mind, so you may feel something before you realise what it is.

This aura is connected to your heart chakra (see page 47).

The Etheric Body

This blue layer (see page 10) is where we are at our most intuitive – and, in some cases, psychic. This layer is what allows us to connect with other people's energy. This connection can be particularly profound if you are literally on the same wavelength as someone else, able to communicate almost without words, but even if you aren't, this auric energy will help you communicate better.

This aura is connected to your throat chakra (see page 45).

The Celestial Body

Here we store our most creative thoughts and ideas; this is the indigo layer (see page 10), which is the level of enlightenment, of accessing the subconscious. This level is often very strong in creative people, who can see things differently and are then able to make manifest their dreams in material form.

This aura is connected to your third-eye chakra (see page 43).

The Causal Body

This violet level (see page 10) harmonises all the others and is the focus of inspiration for your life's path. Like the penetrating and rotating beam of light from a lighthouse, it's as if this aura is looking beyond the physical to make its connections. It also links past experience to the future, and accessing this can often remove emotional blocks in your path.

This aura is connected to your crown chakra (see page 41).

Aura Colours

The colours we see in the world around us are made up of different vibrating frequencies, a form of energy that we can actually see. When a prism splits white colour into the seven colours of the rainbow, we can see that they follow a particular energetic order. Colours with lower vibrational frequencies include the warmer hues of red and orange, while blue colours have a cooler energy with higher vibrational frequencies. The highest energy frequency comes from deep purple and indigo colours, those associated with spirituality.

The chromatic variation of colour, which can include mixed colours (like red and green to create brown), will also affect the energy spectrum. When working with auras, the different colours can appear muddied or faint, and this can indicate intensity or deficiencies in the energy emitted.

Purple/White

A purple aura is linked to spiritual enlightenment and divine connection. It is unusual to meet someone who is so completely evolved that their aura is white (see page 38).

Indigo

Indigo represents intuition, which anyone can develop, or even a connection to spirituality or a higher consciousness.

Blue

A calm colour, blue is also about communication and an ability to listen. Those with blue auras often instil a feeling of calm in others.

Green

A green aura is associated with healing and growth. Someone who is nurturing and empathetic may well exhibit this colour in their aura.

Yellow

As with any colour, this can vary in intensity, but usually a yellow aura suggests someone optimistic and curious; perhaps they are on an intellectual journey.

Orange

Strongly creative individuals show an orange aura. The more their creativity is expressed, the stronger the colour's intensity. Thwarted creatives may have a paler aura by comparison.

Red

The colour of power and vitality. You can give this aura a boost when you need more physical and emotional strength.

Other colours may also be seen and have a variety of indications that are worth noting. When there is blocked energy, auras may appear as grey and colourless, indicating negativity or a lack of direction. A pink aura indicates affection and open-hearted love; children often have pink auras. A very intense red aura may indicate someone who is frustrated, stressed or angry. A brown aura suggests practicality and someone who is focused on the more material aspects of life. Silvery auras are close to white ones, and are seen in highly intuitive or psychic people. Gold auras are very unusual, appearing almost like a halo, and are a big indicator of connection to spiritual realms.

The Seven Chakras

The seven chakras are the energy centres of the body, and are positioned from the crown of the head to the base of the spine. Chakras control the flow of energy within the body, while auras show the state of different energies around the body. So if you want to power up the energy of your aura, focusing on one – or all – of the chakras will help you to enhance and rebalance it.

Chakra translates as 'wheel', giving the sense of a rotating energy that can become blocked or stagnant, and may sometimes be in need of revitalisation and rebalancing. Working with the chakras is a feature of Kundalini yoga, where the postures and breathwork are all designed to harmonise the energy of the chakras. The ultimate aim is to work at opening the chakras, allowing their energy to flow freely, connecting mind, body and spirit.

The colours of the chakras correspond to those of the rainbow, with all the energy of clear light that has been split by a prism: red, orange, yellow, green, blue, indigo and violet – colours that are also present in our auras, as we have seen. When someone manages a state of complete balance and vitalisation in body, mind and spirit, they reach a state of sublime being and their aura may be white. For most of us, however, the aim is to become aware of our energy states, and rebalance and revitalise them in support of our aura.

The seven chakras of the body also correspond to different crystal vibrations, which you can utilise in your practice to rebalance and boost different areas of energy.

Crown Chakra

SPIRITUALITY

This chakra is sited on the top of the head, and is where we connect to our higher purpose and enlightenment. Its colour, purple, is the colour of spirituality. If this chakra becomes stagnant or blocked, it makes it difficult to keep an open mind and we can become restricted in our thinking.

Associated colour
Violet

Crystals that resonate with this chakra's energy
Amethyst and clear quartz

Third-eye Chakra

AWARENESS

Through this chakra, sited in the middle of the forehead, we can see how things are, both literally and metaphorically, bringing us to a state of awareness and understanding of our path in life, helping us feel aligned to our higher purpose and showing us how to achieve it.

Associated colour
Indigo

Crystals that resonate with this chakra's energy
Lapis lazuli and moonstone

Throat Chakra

COMMUNICATION

This chakra is located in the centre of the throat, in the same position as your larynx or voice box. When this chakra becomes blocked, it's hard to know how to express ourselves or speak out, and we can become defensive in our communication with others.

Associated colour
Blue

Crystals that resonate with this chakra's energy
Aquamarine and turquoise

Heart Chakra

LOVE AND HEALING

Located in the centre of the chest, just next to the heart, this chakra is the seat of compassion for ourselves and others. If we are at peace with ourselves, we can extend our compassion into the world, and open our hearts to receive its love in return.

Associated colour
Green

Crystals that resonate with this chakra's energy
Rose quartz and aventurine

Solar Plexus Chakra

WISDOM AND POWER

Located in the physical area of the stomach, where we hold so many strong emotions. When we connect to this energy, we become more powerful in our ambitions and in our ability to achieve them. This chakra's focus can help us realize our goals.

Associated colour
Yellow

Crystals that resonate with this chakra's energy
Topaz and citrine

Sacral Chakra

CREATIVITY AND SEXUALITY

Located in the lower abdomen and sexual organs, the sacral chakra is the seat of creativity in all its forms, including the creation of new human life. This is a wonderful energy that can free us from old restraints and help us to make new and meaningful connections.

Associated colour
Orange

Crystals that resonate with this chakra's energy
Amber and carnelian

Root Chakra

TRUST

At the very base of the spine, literally where we sit, the energy of the root chakra helps us to connect to what grounds us, and to make the progress we seek. This potent energy also helps us trust in our own powerful chakras that support us in our efforts to think, understand, speak, love and create.

Associated colour
Red

Crystals that resonate with this chakra's energy
Obsidian and tourmaline

PART

✦ II ✦

The Magic of Auras

The energy state of the seven auras is yours to access; this metaphorical magic is in your hands. The energy of light, in its pure white form, is refracted into different wavelengths, energy levels and colours. Refraction involves a change in direction – and you can change the direction in which your energy travels, ensuring it is focused on your higher purpose and works to your advantage. You can ignore this potential in your life, or you can choose to connect to it – and, by extension, to the energy and life force of the universe. This magic is available to everyone with an open heart and an open mind.

Aura Readings

Some people are naturally receptive to auras and see them quite easily. For most of us, however, it's something we can learn.

Once you have identified your own aura and your dominant chakra, you can power it up or calm it down, to help you align your higher purpose with your personal dreams. Bear in mind that the colour and intensity of auras in the same person can fluctuate, depending on their physical, mental or spiritual focus at any one time.

Don't underestimate the importance of sensing colour as well as actually seeing it. We are sensory beings and unconsciously rely on the information we see, hear, smell or touch. Bringing that unconscious recognition into use is a feature of intuition or extra-sensory perception. This is less mystical than it might first sound; it's about using our intuition in the same way we use our other senses, in order to gain insights about ourselves and others.

Sensing and Seeing Your Aura

Visiting a professional aura reader may be a useful first step to guide you into this work. Alternatively, you could have an aura photograph (also known as a Kirlian photograph) taken that shows the colours of your aura, but it's not essential.

Once you understand the basic principles outlined in Part One, there are some quite straightforward things you can do to identify and work with your own aura.

One way to see your aura is by looking at your reflection in the mirror, but using your peripheral vision (if you wear glasses, take them off) rather than staring intently at your own face. Be patient and wait until you see the shift in energy around your image and the colour of your aura emerge.

You can also see your aura by rubbing your hands together. You have a chakra point in the palm of each hand that corresponds to your crown chakra. Energising this point can provide access to your individual aura, which you should see as a distinct colour in the space between your hands as you hold them no more than an inch apart.

Sit quietly in an upright position, somewhere you won't be disturbed (turn off any notifications on your computer or phone). Sit here for at least 15 minutes.

✦

Close your eyes and concentrate on regulating your breath until you feel calm and centred.

✦

Rub your hands together, palm to palm, until they feel warm, to activate the chakra points in each hand.

✦

Hold your hands away from your body, in front of your heart chakra, with the palms facing each other with a small gap between them. Focus on the space between your palms until you see a shift in the colour that surrounds your hands.

Bear in mind that seeing the colour of your aura takes practice and concentration, and also requires an open mind that can connect with the body's energy.

Cleansing and Activating Your Aura

If your aura has become weak, dissipated, unbalanced or generally inaccessible, it can be helpful to cleanse and activate it. Negative vibes can affect us all, and on some days we're more prone to these than others. There are several ways in which you can cleanse your aura, and it's also useful to do this before focusing on doing any work necessary to boost its energy. Try the following, and look to integrate these practices into your daily life to ensure your aura energy remains powered up, so you can tap in to it whenever it's useful to you.

BATHING

When your body is surrounded by water, either in a bath or shower, or while swimming in a natural body of water, you can make a connection with the external layer of your body more easily. The feeling of containment that being in close contact with water can provide will also help you to connect to a spiritual level of energy, particularly if you want to make that connection to a corresponding chakra and its effect on a specific aura.

PHYSICAL EXERCISE

✦

Whether you go for a walk, a run or participate in a yoga session, activating the body is an excellent way of gearing up your sense of yourself as a physically functioning whole being, where your mind, body and spirit are all connected. You cannot fail to be energised at all levels by physical activity.

BREATHWORK

✦

Breathwork engages and connects your body and mind, and can be used in exercise or meditation. Familiarise yourself with how to manage your breath and use it to activate the parasympathetic nervous system, which will also help to ground your energy.

GROUNDING

Grounding is an extension of physical mindfulness. If energy is dissipated and hard to focus, your ability to make the best use of it will be sapped. Seek to ground energies accessed by exercise and breathwork by walking barefoot, preferably on the earth, to connect your energy to and sync with the earth's electrical energy. You can also visualise this connection by repeating the mantra, 'I am grounded.'

USING CRYSTALS

Crystals can be useful in focusing energy. Every crystal has its own vibrational energy, and it's worth finding those that most resonate with you, so you can choose them to work with. Look to your birthstone as a starting point, and also those crystals that are linked to the chakras you wish to energise.

USING ESSENTIAL OILS

Essential oils can help you use your sense of smell to activate the hypothalamus, a part of the brain that helps to keep the body and mind stable. In this way, different scents can help invigorate, rebalance or refresh your chakra and aura energies, depending on the properties of the oil you use and your response to it.

VISUALISATION

Visualisation can be a powerful part of opening up your aura's energy, especially if you can't 'see' what is causing a block or stagnation. Alongside exercise and breathwork, you can actively visualise a stronger, brighter aura surrounding you by imagining yourself in a calm, restorative environment, and asking for and receiving the support you need.

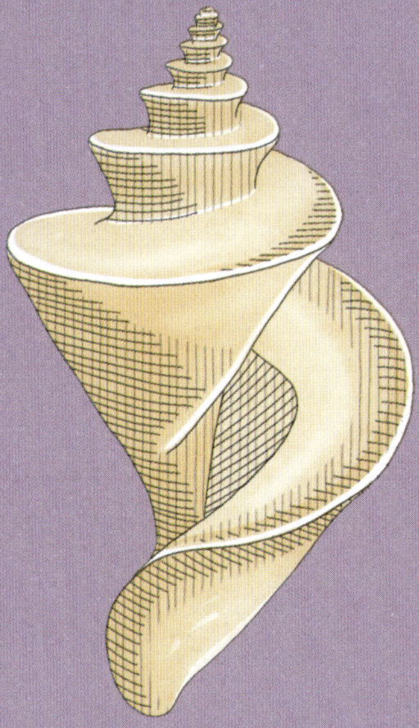

How to Boost Your Aura Energy

Once you have discovered the colour of your aura, you will know what your auric profile is. Are you a creative orange? A healing green? A communicative blue? An intuitive purple? Start with what aura you are, but know that you can link with another should you need its energy. Chakras (see page 37) control the flow of energy within the body, while auras show the state of different energies around the body, so you can use the relevant chakra energy centre to boost its associated aura.

Whether you want to boost your aura in the pursuit of love, work success, social confidence or better health, it's worth spending some time planning rituals that resonate with you and can support your efforts. The following suggestions for different areas on which you might want to focus are designed to get you on the right track, but if you trust your intuition about what your body, mind and spirit might need, you'll soon evolve your own practice.

Remember, when you do this chakra/aura work, your intention is to use a particular energy centre (the chakra) to restore or revitalise your energy state (aura). At any time at which you feel you need support or protection, you can visualise the relevant colour surrounding you to ground or power up your energy.

When working with chakra and aura energy, it's worth considering that if there are areas in your life that need attention and involve other people – your parents, your lover, your child, your work colleagues or your boss, for example – then knowing their aura as well as your own means you can work in harmony with it. You can also use this information to assess their state. For example, if their energy looks or feels depleted, you might want to wait another day to tackle an issue.

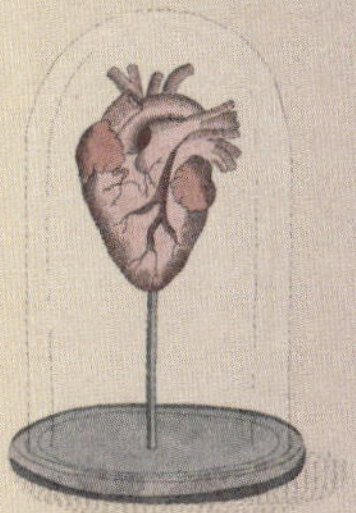

BOOSTING YOUR AURA FOR

LOVE

For this, your focus is on the aura of the astral body and the heart chakra, and your aim is to open up or harmonise the connection between the two. To do this, some breathwork and visualisation are key.

Begin by ensuring you are sitting somewhere quiet, warm and comfortable.

✦

Place your left hand on your heart and your right just below it, on your abdomen.

✦

Close your eyes and visualise a warm pink colour surrounding your body and vibrating with a gentle energy.

✦

Breathe through your nose to engage with your breath. On the inhalation, imagine your heart opening and, on the exhalation, allow that love to flow out into the light surrounding your body.

CRYSTALS FOR LOVE

✦

You can also use a favourite crystal or a piece of rose quartz to enhance this process. Hold the crystal to your heart chakra as you visualise the energy flowing both to and from you, with love.

BOOSTING YOUR AURA FOR

LUCK

How might increasing your general awareness improve your luck? Both the third-eye chakra and the celestial body aura are linked to intuition and imagination, and your intuition and imagination can help you to make unusual connections, yielding interesting results that create your own luck. When this chakra and aura are in harmony, you may find yourself instinctively making lucky choices or creating situations where luck can happen for you.

To improve your focus on increasing your luck, try visualising a deep blue or indigo colour surrounding you.

✦

Take some time to practise gratitude for all the good things that have already happened; this mindfulness will help open your awareness to future possibilities, revealing the steps you've taken in the past that helped to create the luck you've enjoyed.

CRYSTALS FOR LUCK

✦

You can also use a piece of lapis lazuli as a focus for your meditation, as this crystal's energy resonates with the celestial body aura and third-eye chakra.

BOOSTING YOUR AURA FOR

WORK

Becoming more emotionally intelligent at work can help boost your success, and working with the mental body aura and solar plexus chakra can give you this edge. Harmonising the two can open up new channels of wisdom and power, both of which are extremely valuable in the workplace and when you are dealing with colleagues, clients or your boss.

You can help power up this energy through exercise and breathwork, and these can be further revitalised by the colour yellow and exercising in sunshine.

✦

Even a sun salutation yoga routine before work will be helpful in your pursuit of career success.

CRYSTALS FOR WORK

✦

You may also find the crystals citrine and topaz help you focus on this, so keeping either of these in your workspace can be beneficial.

BOOSTING YOUR AURA FOR

CREATIVITY

Creativity is a key component of success in many areas of life: in your work, in your artistic endeavours and in your relationships. Staying curious and open to life's opportunities also fuels creativity, so focus on your sacral chakra, the seat of pleasure that supports creativity. This will help open up the connectivity of the emotional body aura to remove any emotional restraints that could stop you realising your full creative potential.

Boosting this aura is all about emotional connectivity, so seek this out by enjoying the work of other creatives, perhaps by attending concerts, art galleries, theatres and cinemas. In short, engage with anything that can fuel your own creativity.

✦

The colour orange strongly resonates with this energy. Visualise yourself surrounded by this colour, or seek out orange items to wear or have around you.

CRYSTALS FOR CREATIVITY

✦

Both amber and carnelian resonate with sacral chakra energy, and you can use both to focus you when you wish to meditate on your next creative step.

BOOSTING YOUR AURA FOR

COMMUNICATION

Good communication takes confidence, willingness to listen, and the ability to harness your own thoughts. You can work on your confidence separately (see page 102), but when it comes to communication, your focus should be on opening your throat chakra and using this to boost your etheric body aura. You can feel when your throat chakra is blocked, as your actual voice may feel restricted, making it difficult to talk (communicate).

The calm, collected colour blue is your friend here, and visualising this shade or focusing on something blue when you want to open this chakra is a good first step.

✦

This can include gazing up at a lovely blue sky or enjoying the blue of a glass or ceramic object.

CRYSTALS FOR COMMUNICATION

✦

Aquamarine and turquoise crystals can also help to enhance your focus on boosting your communication energy.

BOOSTING YOUR AURA FOR

HEALTH

Physical, mental and spiritual health are closely linked, and it pays to give all your regular attention. All work done with specific chakras and auras is a subtle interplay; here, the physical body aura and root chakra are your focus.

Exercise that is good for your physical health must be balanced with the rest and recuperation needed for your mental health.

✦

A competitive game of tennis can heighten your energy, but it can also tire you. Remember to alternate high-impact exercise with restorative yoga or a gentle walk.

✦

Pay attention to the colour red. This shade can energise you, but it can also overwhelm, so this needs consideration.

CRYSTALS FOR HEALTH

✦

The crystals obsidian and tourmaline can help you to balance this energy and avoid burnout.

BOOSTING YOUR AURA FOR

CONFIDENCE

When you feel mentally strong, it's easier to feel confident, and for this you need to access the rationality of the mental body aura by opening up the solar plexus chakra.

If you have an event coming up that's making you feel nervous and you feel you need a confidence boost, try this ritual the night before to help you relax and sleep. You can also re-engage with it just before the event to boost its impact. Close your eyes as you regulate your breath, visualising the colour yellow surrounding you and imagining your aura powering up with this optimistic and confident energy.

✦

Physical exercise can also be helpful to use up and rebalance nervous energy, and to help you deepen your breath to your abdomen to centre your energy.

CRYSTALS FOR CONFIDENCE

✦

You may also find the energy of the crystals citrine and topaz help you return to a centred state more easily if you keep these with you during the day.

BOOSTING YOUR AURA FOR

SEX

Sex between two people can be a creative act that links body, mind and spirit – but it can also be something more mundane, limited and transactional. If this is what has evolved for you, you might want to change things by powering up your emotional body aura and sacral chakra.

Work on your own sexual energy first, as this will make you more receptive to your partner's and more confident about communicating with them.

✦

The colour orange resonates with this energy, so visualise being surrounded by it or using it in your surroundings.

✦

Once you have worked on your own sexual energy, you may be able to involve your partner in this focus, perhaps through foreplay. You can also use breathwork or essential oils in massage oil to enhance the energy and connection between you.

CRYSTALS FOR SEX

✦

Amber and carnelian are the crystals that resonate with this chakra's energy.

Acknowledgements

First and foremost, thanks are due to my inspirational and creative publisher Kate Pollard, who is always willing to go the extra mile to produce books of substance and beauty, and to Sofie Shearman for her good humour and editorial skills. Thanks are also due to illustrator Lucy Pollard and the design team at Evi-O.Studio for creating such a gorgeous series of books.

About the Author

Gaia Elliot is a green witch based in London. She loves tending to her garden and being surrounded by the abundance of nature, which feeds into her spell-casting and magic-making. Gaia believes that anyone can harness their inner power by tapping in to their intuition. She has a strong interest in tarot, the power of the moon and psychology. Gaia's spiritual journey started when she was a young woman, and she loves nothing more than helping other people to start or continue their own journeys. She is the author of *The Book of Answers*, and the first four books in the *Pocket Mystic* series – *Emergency Spells*, *Manifesting*, *Moon Magic* and *Pendulum Magic*, also published by Quadrille.

Quadrille, Penguin Random House UK, One Embassy Gardens,
8 Viaduct Gardens, London SW11 7BW

Quadrille Publishing Limited is part of the Penguin Random House group of companies whose addresses can be found at global.penguinrandomhouse.com

Penguin Random House UK

Published by Quadrille in 2025
www.penguin.co.uk

A CIP catalogue record for this book is available from the British Library

ISBN 978-183783-397-9
10 9 8 7 6 5 4 3 2 1

Managing Dierctor: Sarah Lavelle
Publishing Director: Kate Pollard
Editor: Sofie Shearman
Design and Art Direction: Evi-O.Studio
Illustrator: Lucy Pollard
Production Controller: Martina Georgieva

Colour reproduction by p2d

Printed in China by RR Donnelley Asia Printing Solution Limited

The authorised representative in the EEA is Penguin Random House Ireland, Morrison Chambers, 32 Nassau Street, Dublin D02 YH68.

FSC
MIX
Paper | Supporting responsible forestry
FSC® C018179

Penguin Random House is committed to a sustainable future for our business, our readers and our planet. This book is made from Forest Stewardship Council® certified paper.